I can Sa
Prayer

Written and compiled by Sophie Piper
Illustrated by Emily Bolam

LION
CHILDREN'S

contents

I can
find a quiet place

"When you pray," said Jesus,
"go to your room,
close the door,
and pray to your Father God.

"You cannot see your Father God,
but he will see you
and he will bless you."

From Matthew 6:6

I'm sitting
and thinking
and wondering
and wishing
and dreaming
and hoping
and praying

and hoping
and dreaming
and truly
believing
that God
can hear all
that I'm saying.

I can count my fingers

This is my prayer number 1:
bless the day that's just begun.

This is my prayer number 2:
may the sky be clear and blue.

This is my prayer number 3:
God, please take good care of me.

This is my prayer number 4:
help me love you more and more.

This is my prayer number 5:
make me glad to be alive.

This is my prayer number 6:
help me when I'm in a fix.

This is my prayer number 7:
make this world a bit like heaven.

This is my prayer number 8:
put an end to hurt and hate.

This is my prayer number 9:
let the light of kindness shine.

This is my prayer number 10:
bring me safe to bed again.

I can wash with water

I wash my hands
to make them clean
and ready to do good.

And God above
will teach me how
to do the things I should.

I lift my hands to the golden sun:
A shining day has just begun.
I wave my hand to heaven above:
May God protect me with his love.

11

I can
do a good deed

Hands to work
and hands to play,
hands to help
in every way.

Hand to clap
and hands to pray,
hands to praise God
every day.

May my hands be helping hands
For all that must be done
That fetch and carry, lift and hold
And make the hard jobs fun.

May my hands be clever hands
In all I make and do
With sand and dough and clay and things
With paper, paint and glue.

May my hands be gentle hands
And may I never dare
To poke and prod and hurt and harm
But touch with love and care.

13

I can
make music

Sing to God with thankfulness,
sing a song of praise,
sing out loud and joyfully,
sing out all your days.

From Psalm 95

Praise God on the noisy drum
Rumpty tumpty tumpty tum.

Praise God with a mighty clash
Let the cymbals crash-a-bash.

Praise God on the gentle flute
Tootle tootle tootle toot.

Praise God as you pluck the strings
Tring a ling a ling a ling.

Play the trumpet, rum pah pah
May your praises sound afar.

From Psalm 150

I can share a meal

Let us take a moment
To thank God for our food,
For friends around the table
And everything that's good.

Let us say
A thank you prayer
For the food
That's here to share.

The harvest of our garden
is astonishingly small;
but oh, dear God, we thank you
that there's anything at all.

I can walk on the path

I will choose the narrow path,
I will walk the straight,
through the wide and winding world
up to heaven's gate.

18

Ready for sun
and ready for rain
and ready for all kinds of
    weather;
ready to hold
the hand of God
as we all go out together.

19

I can
be kind to animals

Baby creatures, just awakened,
You are part of God's creation;
Baby creatures, oh, so small,
God is father of us all.

We can do no great things
Only small things with great love.

Mother Teresa of Calcutta (1910–97)

Dear Father, hear and bless
your beasts and singing birds;
and guard with tenderness
small things that have no words.

Edith Rutter Leatham (1870–1939)

21

I can
look closely

I think the butterfly
says her prayer
by simply fluttering
in the air.

I think the prayer
of the butterfly
just dances up
to God on high.

Thank you for the little things
we notice every day
that shine on earth
with heaven's gold
and cheer us on our way.

I can
see the night sky

God has counted the stars in the heavens,
God has counted the leaves on the tree;
God has counted the children on earth:
I know God has counted me.

I'm standing here upon the earth
and looking to the sky.
I'm trusting that my quiet prayers
can reach to God on high.

May my life shine
like a star in the night,
filling my world
with goodness and light.

From Philippians 2:15

25

I can kneel down

I am little
I am lowly
God is great and
God is holy;

yet was born
a child like me
here on earth
for all to see;

came from heaven –
great and holy –
to a stable:
little, lowly.

I kneel down to pray:
as I make myself small,
I remember God's greatness.

I bow my head to pray:
as I make myself humble,
I remember God's kindness.

From Psalm 95

I can
say a prayer

"When you pray," said Jesus,
"do not use a lot of words.
Your Father God already knows
what you need before you ask him.

"This, then, is what you should pray:

28

"Our Father in heaven,
hallowed be your name,
your kingdom come,
your will be done,
on earth as in heaven.
Give us today our daily bread.
Forgive us our sins
as we forgive those who sin against us.
Lead us not into temptation
but deliver us from evil.

"For the kingdom,
the power,
and the glory are yours
now and for ever.
Amen."